On second thoughts . . .

GARY BELSKY

Michaél O'Mara Books Limited

First published in Great Britain in 1999 by
Michael O'Mara Books Limited
9 Lion Yard
Tremadoc Road
London SW4 7NQ

First published in the United States in 1999 by
Adams Media Corporation
260 Center Street, Holbrook, MA 02343

A CIP catalogue record for this book is available from the British Library

ISBN 1-85479-467-1

1 3 5 7 9 10 8 6 4 2

Designed and typeset by Keystroke, Wolverhampton

Printed and bound in Great Britain by Cox & Wyman, Reading, Berks

To my old friend Josh Kosowsky, who predicted that this book would never be published

and

To my nephews and niece – Ari, Mo, Adir, Sam, Zevi, and Elly – whom I've loved since they were born, without second thoughts.

Introduction

Eating crow. Eating your words. Foot-in-mouth disease. By any name, we've all experienced it: a promise made, a prediction proffered, or a pronouncement intoned that not only turned out to be false but helped us look like complete fools in the process. This book is an attempt to collect some of the more famous – and infamous – of these verbal miscues in history, ranging from serious miscalculations about life and death to sublime errors about love and romance. It's meant to inform and entertain, but if it helps you feel better about your own verbal gaffes, so much the better.

Isn't it Romantic

"I love him better every day."

Elizabeth Taylor, 1950, just after marrying her first husband, hotel baron Conrad Hilton.

"I just want to be with him, to be his wife."

Elizabeth Taylor, 1952, just before marrying her second husband, actor Michael Wilding.

“Thirty or forty years.”

Elizabeth Taylor, 1959, predicting the length of her honeymoon to fourth husband, singer Eddie Fisher. (Her third husband, Michael Todd, died in a plane crash one year after their 1957 marriage.)

“This marriage will last forever.”

Elizabeth Taylor, 1964, at her marriage to fifth husband Richard Burton, whom she divorced in 1974.

"We are stuck together like chicken feathers to tar."

Elizabeth Taylor, 1975, discussing her remarriage to Richard Burton, which lasted a year.

"I have never been so happy."

Elizabeth Taylor, 1976, soon after marrying Senator John Warner.

"This is it, forever."

Elizabeth Taylor, 1991, announcing her marriage to Larry Fortensky, which ended in 1995.

"If any couple is in love, they'll have a happy marriage and no amount of gossip will ever break it up."

Movie starlet Janet Leigh, 1953, denying reports that her marriage to Tony Curtis was in trouble. The couple divorced in 1962.

"Don't pay any attention to any of the drivel you hear about me and Jack Kennedy. It doesn't mean a thing."

Jackie Bouvier, 1952, to then-fiancé John Husted. A year later she married Kennedy.

"I got you babe."

Husband and wife song team Sonny and Cher, 1965–1974, who sang their hit song at the end of each episode of their weekly variety show – until the show was cancelled in the wake of their 1974 divorce.

"Rod will stay with me – forever."

Actress Britt Ekland, 1976, on her husband, rock star Rod Stewart. Forever lasted a year before the couple divorced in 1977.

"I couldn't have married any other kind of woman."

Prince Charles, 1991, on his doomed marriage to Lady Diana Spencer. Perhaps he should have.

"Now I have what I always wanted . . . I have my knight in shining armour."

Former Miss America Phyllis George, 1981, on her marriage to Kentucky governor John Y. Brown Jr. By 1996, the armour had rusted and the Browns divorced.

"Where I am now is where I will remain for the rest of my life. The family is solid."

Actress Jane Fonda, 1984, on her marriage to Tom Hayden. Fonda is now wed to US media mogul Ted Turner.

"I simply want to be a family man."

Singer Elton John, 1984, upon his marriage to sound engineer Renate Blauel. The couple divorced four years later, and John soon after announced to no surprise that he was, in fact, gay.

"It's so wonderful at last to have found someone to look after me."

Sarah, Duchess of York, 1986, on her ill-fated marriage to Prince Andrew.

" . . . the coolest guy in the universe."

Album dedication from Madonna, 1986, to her husband, the actor Sean Penn, less than three years before she filed for divorce.

"I feel like Cinderella. I married Prince Charming."

Actress Loni Anderson, 1988, upon marrying actor Burt Reynolds, whom she divorced in a bitter fight five years later.

"I'm married to the greatest man in the world."

Designer Carolyne Roehm, 1990, on her husband, tycoon Henry Kravis, three years before their divorce.

"I just knew she was the one for me. My happiness is complete."

Charles, the 9th Earl Spencer, circa 1990, on his reason for asking model Victoria Lockwood to marry him after knowing her just ten days. They later divorced.

"This is what we call paradise."

Actor Cotter Smith, 1990, on his wedded bliss with actress Mel Harris. Paradise ended in 1996.

"Why go looking when you already have exactly what you want?"

Tycoon Donald Trump, summer 1991, on his reconciliation with girlfriend Marla Maples.

"It's the end of an era."

Donald Trump, autumn 1991, on breaking up with Marla Maples again, before getting back together with her two weeks later. The couple eventually married, but filed for divorce in 1997.

"This is completely right."

Actress Julia Roberts, 1993, on her twenty-one-month marriage to singer Lyle Lovett.

"Christie Brinkley loves me now. What else do I need?"

Singer Billy Joel, 1993, a year before he and Brinkley split up.

". . . it really is like Cinderella."

Pop music star Mariah Carey, 1993, on her marriage to record mogul Tommy Mottola. Four years later she split from Prince Charming.

"He's always been the fun I never had in my life."

Actress Roseanne Barr, March 1993, describing husband Tom Arnold – before the fun ended and she divorced him.

"I care about being with my husband. I take my marriage seriously."

Actress Shannen Doherty, January 1994 – four months after marrying actor Ashley Hamilton, and three months before filing for divorce.

"The best thing I've ever done in my whole life."

Actress Pamela Anderson Lee, 1995, on her marriage to rock star Tommy Lee, a year before filing for divorce. Anderson Lee changed her mind again – and then again, filing for divorce in February 1998.

"Incredibly monogamous."

Opera singer Luciano Pavarotti, October 1995, describing his marriage to Adua Pavarotti. Less than half a year later Pavarotti admitted to having an affair with a twenty-six-year-old assistant.

"I've found the person I'm complete with."

Actress Gwyneth Paltrow, autumn 1996, discussing her soon-to-be fiancé Brad Pitt. Less than a year later the couple had broken up.

MONKEY BUSINESS

"There has never been a time in our history when work was so abundant, or when wages were as high."

President Grover Cleveland, January 1893. Within months the United States was in the throes of depression.

"The horse is here to stay, but the automobile is only a novelty – a fad."

The president of the Michigan Savings Bank advising Henry Ford's lawyer Horace Rackham not to invest in the Ford Motor Company, 1903.

"We may look with confidence to the progress of business in 1929."

International Business Machines founder Thomas Watson, 1928, less than a year before the stock market crashed and the United States swooned into depression.

"I think there is a world market for about five computers."

IBM chairman Thomas Watson, 1943.

"The concept is interesting and well-formed, but in order to earn better than a 'C' the idea must be feasible."

Yale University management professor's comment on a paper written by Fred Smith proposing an overnight delivery service, *circa* early 1970s. Smith went on to start Federal Express.

"What's it good for?"

Intel chairman and co-founder Gordon Moore, early 1970s, when presented with the idea for personal computers.

"This is like trying to buy a ticket on the *Titanic*."

New York real-estate developer Fred Trump, 1976, on his son Donald's plan to buy the failing Commodore Hotel in Manhattan. In fact, the successful deal launched Donald's career.

"There is no reason for any individual to have a computer in their home."

Digital Equipment president Ken Olsen, 1977.

"The most significant soft drink development in the company's history. The best has been made even better."

Coca-Cola chairman Roberto Goizueta, 1985, on New Coke®. It was pulled from store shelves three months later.

"The force in this country buying high-yield securities [junk bonds] has overpowered all regulation."

Wall Street financier and junk-bond king Michael Milken, 1986, less than four years before government regulation overpowered and sent him to prison.

"No ifs, ands, or buts, Lou, it's going up."

Financial pundit Dan Dorfman to CNN anchor Lou Dobbs, October 1987 – the night before a four-day, 769-point slide in the stock market.

"If the [Texas savings-and-loan, equivalent to building societies] industry is to survive, its member institutions must take positive steps to rebuild public confidence by instituting strict codes of ethical business conduct."

American Federal Bank chairman William E. Gibson, 1989, three years before he was convicted in federal court of fraud.

"[Tonya] Harding and her down-home All-American appeal and charm will knock the winter socks off many Americans. Add to this that she is a young woman and happily married and you have an excellent spokesperson for family oriented products and services."

Press release from the consulting firm Sports Marketing Group, October 1991. Ms Harding's husband later admitted assaulting her chief skating rival, Nancy Kerrigan.

"[I am] prepared to be a full-time chairman of Apple. I am not walking away from Apple. I have no plans to go anywhere else."

Apple Computer chairman John Sculley, June 1993, four months before quitting his post to take another job.

"It was a gem that fell into my lap."

Former Apple chairman John Sculley, October 1993, describing his decision to take over tiny Spectrum Technologies – four months before resigning from the company.

"It's difficult to see how stocks can move much higher."

Former Lehman Brothers market strategist Katherine Hensel, January 1995. In fact, stock prices increased more than 20 per cent that year and the next.

"I am especially gratified to be able to have an additional partner going forward to manage this great and complex entertainment company. There's plenty for the two of us to do."

Disney chairman Michael Eisner, August 1995, commenting on the hiring of superagent Michael Ovitz as company president. Within eighteen months Ovitz resigned and Eisner called his hiring a mistake.

Inexact Science

"Inventions reached their limit long ago, and I see no hope for further development."

Julius Frontinus, first century AD.

“So many centuries after creation, it is unlikely that anyone could find hitherto unknown lands of any value.”

From a report presented to King Ferdinand V and Queen Isabella of Spain, 1486, regarding Christopher Columbus’s plan to search for a shorter route to the Indies.

“The western ocean is infinite and perhaps unnavigable.”

From the same report, 1486.

"Men might as well project a voyage to the moon as attempt to employ steam navigation against the stormy north Atlantic Ocean."

Irish astronomer, philosopher and professor Dionysius Lardner, 1838.

"Rail travel at high speed is not possible, because passengers, unable to breathe, would die of asphyxia."

Irish astronomer, philosopher, and professor Dionysius Lardner, *circa* 1835.

"Drill for oil? You mean drill into the ground and try to find oil? You're crazy!"

Response from drilling company executives to oil industry pioneer Edwin Drake, 1859.

"Louis Pasteur's theory of germs is ridiculous fiction."

French professor of physiology Pierre Pachet, 1872.

"The telephone has too many shortcomings to be seriously considered as a means of communication."

A corporate memo from telegraph operator Western Union, 1876.

"What use could this company make of an electric toy?"

Western Union president William Orton, *circa* 1870s, turning down the chance to buy Alexander Graham Bell's patent for the telephone.

"The abdomen, the chest, and the brain will forever be shut from the intrusion of the wise and humane."

Sir John Eric Erichsen, Surgeon-Extraordinary to Queen Victoria, predicting in the early 1870s that surgery would never succeed.

"Railroads, water courses, telegraphs, telephones, pneumatic tubes, and all other methods of transporting passengers, freight, and intelligence will be owned and operated by the government."

American labour leader T.V. Powderly, 1893, predicting the role of government a hundred years in the future.

"I presume that, in the next century, there may be built a railway reaching so far that it may be possible to enter a palace car in New York City and ride it to Lima, Santiago, Rio de Janeiro, or Buenos Aires."

Famed US industrialist W.R. Grace, 1893.

"Heavier-than-air flying machines are impossible."

British mathematician and physicist William Thomson Kelvin, 1895.

“Everything that can be invented, has been invented.”

US Patent Office commissioner Charles Duell, 1899.

“I must confess that my imagination . . . refuses to see any sort of submarine doing anything but suffocating its crew and floundering at sea.”

British author and futurist H.G. Wells, 1901.

“Man will not fly for fifty years.”

Aviation pioneer Wilbur Wright, 1901.

“The aeroplane will never fly.”

British minister of war Lord Haldane, 1907.

“Flight by machines heavier than air is unpractical and insignificant.”

Astronomer Simon Newcomb, 1907, eighteen months before the Wright brothers’ first flight.

“No flying machine will *ever* fly from New York to Paris.”

Orville Wright, 1908.

"Aeroplanes are interesting toys but of no military value."

French military strategist Ferdinand Foch, 1911.

"The popular mind often pictures gigantic flying machines speeding across the Atlantic, carrying innumerable passengers.
. . . Such ideas must be wholly visionary. Even if such a machine could get across with one or two passengers, it would be prohibitive to any but the capitalist who could own his own yacht."

Harvard astronomer William Pickering, 1913.

"[Airmail is] an impractical sort of fad, and has no place in the serious job of postal transportation."

Second Assistant US Postmaster-General
Paul Henderson, 1922.

"Professor Goddard . . . does not know the relation of action to reaction, and of the need to have something better than a vacuum against which to react. . . . Of course, he only seems to lack the knowledge ladled out daily in high schools."

New York Times editorial, 1920, refuting the notion that rocketry pioneer Robert Goddard's inventions could actually travel in outer space.

"[Would it] not be well to exclude women from a field of activity in which [their] presence certainly is unnecessary from any point of view?"

New York Times editorial, 1921, on the question of whether women should be allowed to pilot planes.

"The wireless music box has no imaginable commercial value. Who would pay for a message sent to nobody in particular?"

Response from associates of RCA founder David Sarnoff, *circa* 1920s, when he proposed investing in the young radio industry.

"This fellow Charles Lindbergh will never make it. He's doomed."

Millionaire and aviation buff Harry Guggenheim, 1927, on Lindy's soon-to-be-successful solo flight across the Atlantic.

"This foolish idea of shooting at the moon is an example of the absurd length to which vicious specialization will carry scientists working in thought-tight compartments."

British scientist William Bickerton, 1929.

“The most revolutionary war invention since the discovery of gunpowder.”

An article in the July 1932 issue of *Modern Mechanics*, describing plans to build a flying tank.

“Anyone who expects a source of power from the transformation of the atom is talking moonshine.”

British Nobel laureate and scientist
Lord Rutherford, 1933.

"Automobiles will start to decline almost as soon as the last shot is fired in World War II. . . . Instead of a car in every garage, there will be a helicopter."

Aviation publicist Harry Bruno, 1943.

"RAAF [Roswell Army Air Field] Captures Flying Saucer on Ranch in Roswell Region."

Roswell Daily Record headline, July 8, 1945, one day before the newspaper retracted the fabled hoax.

"Computers in the future may weigh no more than 1.5 tons."

Popular Mechanics, 1949.

"Space travel is utter bilge."

Richard van der Riet Woolley, royal astronomer and space adviser to the British government, 1956. A year later the Russians successfully launched the *Sputnik* satellite.

"A few decades hence, energy may be free, just like the unmetred air."

US Atomic Energy Commission member John von Neumann, 1956, on the impact of nuclear power.

"Man will never reach the moon regardless of all future scientific advances."

Renowned American scientist and inventor Lee De Forest, 1957, twelve years before Neil Armstrong stepped off *Apollo 9* and on to the moon.

"For the majority of people, the use of tobacco has a beneficial effect."

Los Angeles surgeon Ian MacDonald, 1963, as quoted in *Newsweek*.

"But what good is it for?"

Now-anonymous engineer at IBM, 1968, commenting on the recent invention of the microchip.

"640K ought to be good enough for anybody."

Microsoft president Bill Gates, 1981, on the sufficiency of computer memory at the time.

Politically Incorrect

"One should not believe in conspiracies until they have attained their goal."

Roman emperor Domitian, who was assassinated by conspiracists in AD 96.

"In 1993, the government will have grown more simple."

American poet Ella Wheeler Wilcox, 1893.

"Politically, there will be far less money expended in electing officials."

Famed newspaper columnist Bill Nye, 1893, when asked to predict how the U.S. would look in 1993.

"Sensible and responsible women do not want to vote."

Former president Grover Cleveland, 1900, on the suffrage movement.

"Herbert Hoover is certainly a wonder, and I wish we could make him President. There couldn't be a better one."

Franklin D. Roosevelt, 1920, four years before he ran for president – against Hoover.

"I want to be an old-fashioned lawyer, an honest lawyer who can't be bought by crooks."

Future President Richard Nixon, 1925, to his mother.

"A pleasant man who, without any important qualifications for the office, would very much like to be President."

Newspaper columnist Walter Lippmann, 1932, discussing future four-term US President Franklin Delano Roosevelt.

"FDR will be a one-term president."

Newspaper columnist Mark Sullivan, 1935, on the chances of re-election of Franklin D. Roosevelt, who went on to win three more terms in office.

"I have no political ambition for myself or for my children."

Joseph P. Kennedy, 1936.

"There is [*sic*] not enough troops in the army to force the Southern people to break down segregation and admit the Negro race into our theatres, into our swimming pools, and into our churches."

US Senator Strom Thurmond, 1948.

"Dewey Defeats Truman."

Chicago Tribune headline, November 4, 1948.
Actually, Truman defeated Dewey
in that presidential election.

"Castro won't last a year."

Cuban president Fulgencio Batista, 1957.

"Television is not as effective as it once was."

Presidential candidate Richard Nixon, assessing the significance of his televised debates with John F. Kennedy in 1960. Nixon's poor showing in the debates was thought to be his undoing in the election.

"The boy didn't win."

Vice-presidential nominee Lyndon B. Johnson, assessing running mate JFK's debate performance.

"Segregation now! Segregation tomorrow! Segregation forever."

Alabama governor George Wallace, 1963, less than nine months before Alabama schools were integrated.

"I promise that truth shall be the policy of the Nixon administration."

Vice-President Spiro Agnew, 1968.

"Truth will become the hallmark of the Nixon administration."

Director of communications, Executive Branch, US Government, Herb Klein, 1969.

"No woman will in my time be prime minister."

British politician – and future prime minister – Margaret Thatcher, 1969.

"[I'm] 100 per cent for Tom Eagleton . . . [I have] no intention of dropping him from the ticket."

US Senator and Democratic presidential candidate George McGovern, July 1972, denying that he would drop Eagleton as his vice-presidential running mate. He dropped him days later.

"I'm not going to comment from the White House on a third-rate burglary attempt."

White House press secretary Ron Ziegler, 1972, commenting on the burglary of Democratic National Headquarters at the Watergate apartment building.

"The Vice-Presidency is not much of a job."

Nelson Rockefeller, 1974, weeks before accepting Gerald Ford's offer to become Vice-President of the United States.

"I don't want to be prime minister again. It's pretty tough going."

Indira Gandhi, 1974, shortly before she ran for and won the prime minister's job again.

"An island of stability."

President Jimmy Carter, 1979, describing the Shah of Iran, a few months before the Shah was overthrown.

"I would like to suggest that Ronald Reagan is politically dead."

NBC political correspondent Tom Pettit, January 1980.

"If you don't believe me, just follow me."

US presidential hopeful Gary Hart, 1988, denying reports that he was engaged in an adulterous affair. Reporters took his suggestion and discovered his relationship with Donna Rice.

"Read my lips: no new taxes."

George Bush, 1988, eighteen months before he raised taxes and four years before he lost the 1992 election to Bill Clinton.

". . . the fire of an election no longer burns in me."

Arkansas governor Bill Clinton, 1990, explaining why he would not run again for public office.

"I want to say one thing to the American people. I want you to listen to me. I'm going to say this again: I did not have sexual relations with that woman, Miss Lewinsky."

US President Bill Clinton, January 26, 1998.

"I did have a relationship with Miss Lewinsky that was not appropriate. In fact, it was wrong."

Clinton, eight months later.

"We happen to believe, despite the polls, that Bill Clinton will lose to any Republican who doesn't drool on stage."

Wall Street Journal, October 1995.

"The last time I checked, the Constitution said 'of the people, by the people, and for the people.' That's what the Declaration of Independence said."

President Bill Clinton, 1996. Actually, the phrase in question is from Lincoln's Gettysburg Address.

"I share your view that the urgent problem of species extinction and the conservation of biological diversity should be addressed. The first step in saving any plant or animal from extinction is to become aware of and respect the fragile ecosystems that make up our environment."

US Vice-President Al Gore, 1996, in a letter to a Dallas couple who complained about the elimination of the "Texas Eagle". Gore didn't realize the "Texas Eagle" was an Amtrak train connecting Dallas to Chicago and the West Coast.

"I was very clearly asked to do the job of being the chief spokesman for the party. I could not do fund-raising."

US Senator Christopher Dodd, February 1997, two months before he admitted to raising money for the party.

"McKinley has no more backbone than a chocolate eclair."

Theodore Roosevelt, 1898, ridiculing the notion that President William McKinley would go to war against Spain, which he soon after did.

Might Makes Wrong

"Moscow deserted! A most unlikely event."

Napoleon Bonaparte, 1812, before entering the evacuated city, which had been set ablaze by fleeing Russians.

"Our flag still waves proudly from the walls."

US commander at the Alamo W. Barret Travis, 1836, in his last message before his entire garrison was wiped out by Mexican troops.

"There is no doubt that Jefferson Davis and the other leaders of the South have made an army . . . they have made a nation."

Future British prime minister William Gladstone, 1865, shortly before the South collapsed.

"Everyone spoke of the possibility of conflict involving all of Europe, but no one here really believed that such a thing was likely to come about."

New York Times financial columnist, June 1914, describing the mood in Europe after the assassination of Austrian Archduke Franz-Ferdinand. Within a month, World War I had begun.

"You will be home before the leaves have fallen from the trees."

German Kaiser Wilhelm II, August 1914, to his troops at the beginning of World War I, which went on for over four years.

"Bullets have little stopping power against the horse."

British general Sir Douglas Haig, 1914, on the advantages of the cavalry.

“There will be no war.”

President Woodrow Wilson, January 1917, two months before the US entered World War I.

“The culmination and final war for human liberty.”

President Woodrow Wilson, January 1918, predicting that World War I would be the last global war.

"It is about as unthinkable that we should enter armed conflict with our nearest neighbours across the Pacific as it is that we should go to war with one of our nearest neighbours across the Atlantic."

Thomas Lamont, director of the Japan Society of America, speaking in 1928 about the unlikelihood that the US and Japan would ever fight a war.

"Mistreatment of Jews in Germany may be considered virtually eliminated."

US Secretary of State Cordell Hull, 1933. Within a decade, virtually the entire Jewish population of Germany, and Europe, would be destroyed.

"Believe me, Germany is unable to wage war."

Former British prime minister David Lloyd George, 1934.

"Whoever lights the torch of war in Europe can wish for nothing but chaos."

German Chancellor Adolf Hitler, May 1935, dismissing the notion that Germany wanted war.

"Germany has no desire to attack any country in Europe."

Former British prime minister David Lloyd George, 1936.

"A Japanese attack on Pearl Harbor is a strategic impossibility."

American author George Fielding Eliot, 1938.

"I have no more territorial ambitions in Europe."

Adolf Hitler, 1939, three months before invading Poland.

"For the second time in our history, a British Prime Minister has returned from Germany bringing peace with honour. I believe it is peace for our time. . . . Go home and get some sleep."

British Prime Minister Neville Chamberlain, 1938.

"It has been assumed, in my opinion erroneously, that Japan covets these islands."

US General Douglas MacArthur, 1939, ridiculing rumours that Japan would invade the Philippines, which is exactly what happened some two years later.

"An alliance with Germany and Italy . . . what possible meaning could that have?"

Japanese Prince Kinmochi Saionji, 1939. The alliance meant World War II.

"My feeling and belief is that we are not going to have a war. Germany isn't ready for it. . . . I have my own sources of information."

US Senator William E. Borah, ranking Republican member of the Senate Foreign Relations Committee, July 1939, six weeks before Germany invaded Poland.

“In three weeks, England will have her neck wrung like a chicken.”

French military commander Maxime Weygand, June 1940, assessing England's chances in a war against Nazi Germany. Some 250 weeks later, it was the Germans who were defeated.

“I have said this before, but I shall say it again and again and again; your boys are not going to be sent into any foreign wars.”

President Franklin D. Roosevelt, 1940, before the US entered World War II.

"The United States will not be a threat to us for decades."

Adolf Hitler, November 1940.

"No matter what happens, the US Navy is not going to be caught napping."

US Secretary of the Navy Frank Knox, December 4, 1941, three days before the Japanese surprise attack on Pearl Harbor.

"Though neutral during WW II, Switzerland favoured the Allied cause."

Inscription on a watch given in 1946 to President Harry Truman by the citizens of Geneva. In fact, the Swiss helped finance the Nazi war effort.

"No commander in the history of war has had more complete and admirable support than I have during the Korean War."

US General Douglas MacArthur, October 1950, six months before he was fired as head of United Nations forces in Korea.

"We will bury you."

Soviet premier Nikita Khrushchev, 1959, to US Vice-President Richard Nixon.

"We keep a vigil of peace around the world."

US Vice-President Lyndon B. Johnson, May 1963, even as the US was sending "military advisers" to South Vietnam.

"We are not about to send American boys nine or ten thousand miles away from home to do what Asian boys ought to be doing for themselves."

President Lyndon B. Johnson, 1964, on Vietnam.

"Our one desire . . . is that the people of South-East Asia be left in peace to work out their own destinies in their own way."

President Lyndon B. Johnson, 1964, even as he was sending more "military advisers" to Vietnam.

"I believe there is a light at the end of what has been a long and lonely tunnel."

President Lyndon B. Johnson, September 1966, referring to the conflict in Vietnam, seven long and lonely years before it actually ended.

"We have reached an important point when the end begins to come into view."

US General William Westmoreland, November 1967, six years before the actual end of US involvement in Vietnam.

"We will drive them into the sea."

Egyptian President Gamal Abdel Nasser, 1968, referring to the State of Israel.

"I want to see peace and prosperity and happiness in my country, and I think we are going about it in the best way."

Provisional Irish Republican Army leader Joe Cahill, 1971.

Humble Opinions

"Far too noisy, my dear Mozart. Far too many notes."

Austrian Emperor Joseph II, 1786, after hearing the first performance of Mozart's opera *The Marriage of Figaro*.

"We fancy that any real child might be more puzzled than enchanted by this stiff, overwrought story."

Children's Books review of Lewis Carroll's *Alice in Wonderland*, 1865.

"I'm sorry, Mr. Kipling, but you just don't understand how to use the English language."

Publisher's rejection letter, 1889, to *Jungle Book* author Rudyard Kipling.

"This can only end in suicide. One day, Picasso will be found hanging behind the *Demoiselles*."

Painter André Derain, *circa* 1910, on rival Pablo Picasso's *Les Demoiselles d'Avignon*, widely considered to be the renowned painter's breakthrough painting.

"Possibly some might call it a feminist novel . . . but we are sure Miss Cather had nothing so inartistic in mind."

New York Times book review of Willa Cather's *O Pioneers!*, 1913, widely thought to be one of the most important feminist novels ever written.

"So this is a book of the season only."

New York Herald Tribune book review of F. Scott Fitzgerald's *The Great Gatsby*, 1925.

"Who the hell wants to hear actors talk?"

Movie mogul and Warner Brothers founder Harry Warner, 1927.

"Can't act. Can't sing. Balding. Can dance a little."

MGM executive, 1929, about Fred Astaire's screen test.

"*Gone With the Wind* is going to be the biggest flop in Hollywood history."

Gary Cooper, 1937, after turning down the role of Rhett Butler.

"No legs, no jokes, no chance."

Producer Mike Todd, 1943, predicting a quick demise of the new Broadway musical *Oklahoma!*, which played for a then-record 2,212 performances.

“It is impossible to sell animal stories in the USA.”

Publisher’s rejection letter, 1945, of George Orwell’s *Animal Farm.*

“You cannot show a pregnant woman on television.”

Biow Advertising Agency executive, 1953, telling Desi Arnaz that it would be a mistake to have his wife, Lucille Ball, shown pregnant on their show *I Love Lucy*. Little Ricky’s birth, of course, was one of the highest-rated television shows ever.

"You ain't going nowhere . . . son. You ought to go back to driving a truck."

Grand Ole Opry manager Jim Denny, 1954, firing Elvis Presley after one performance.

"With your voice, nobody is going to let you broadcast."

CBS producer Don Hewitt, 1958, to Barbara Walters.

"Any literary merit the book may have is far outweighed by the pornographic and smutty passages."

US Postmaster-General Arthur Summerfield, 1959, banning D.H. Lawrence's *Lady Chatterley's Lover*. A month later, a federal judge overruled his decision.

"There's gotta be a better way to make a living."

Tonight Show host Jack Paar, February 11, 1960, before walking off a live broadcast after just three minutes. A month later Paar returned.

"We don't like their sound. Groups of guitars are on their way out."

Decca Recording Company, 1962, upon turning down The Beatles.

"Reagan doesn't have the presidential look."

United Artists studio executive, 1964.

"The screen soon overflows with so much brotherhood [and] piety [it will make you] retch."

Newsweek magazine, 1964, panning the soon-to-be hit movie *Lilies of the Field*, for which Sidney Poitier became the first black man to win an Oscar for Best Actor.

"They've got their own groups. What are we going to give them that they don't already have?"

Paul McCartney, 1964, anticipating The Beatles' arrival in the USA.

"They know it's a lot of nonsense. [In another month] America will have had its giggle and once more will be worrying about Castro and Khrushchev."

New York Daily News critic Anthony Burton, February 11, 1964, dismissing "Beatlemania".

"Malefic and sick."

New York Times movie critic Bosley Crowther, 1964, reviewing *Dr. Strangelove*, widely considered one of the best films ever made.

"Get rid of the pointed-ears guy."

NBC television executive to *Star Trek* creator Gene Roddenberry, 1966, recommending the new show eliminate the Vulcan character Mr. Spock.

"Psychedelic Uncle Tom."

Esquire magazine review of rock-and-roll legend Jimi Hendrix, 1967.

"It's pretty thin, son. I don't think people will follow it."

Henry Fonda, 1969, commenting to son Peter about his new film – *Easy Rider* – which became an instant hit.

"I assure you Marlon Brando will not appear in this film."

Paramount Studios president Stanley Jaffe, *circa* 1970, on the role of Vito Corleone in *The Godfather*. Brando won an Oscar for his performance in the part.

"Boring and predictable."

Time magazine, 1971, panning the future television hit show *All in the Family*.

"Even an offbeat showcase needs quality."

New York Times review, 1975, panning *Saturday Night Live*.

"We're going to make everybody forget The Beatles."

Bee Gees singer Barry Gibb, 1976, on his group's movie version of the Beatles' *Sgt. Pepper's Lonely Hearts Club Band.*

"I'm fifty now, and I am sure I won't be doing the *Tonight Show* in ten years. I doubt if I'll be doing it at fifty-five."

Johnny Carson, 1976, who stayed on the job until he was sixty-six.

"A flash in the pan."

Billboard magazine, 1983, in a review of Madonna.

"Her involvement has had a very adverse impact on her career because she's unwilling to exploit the situation."

Attorney Larry Stein, 1996, speaking about his client, O.J. Simpson's ex-girlfriend Paula Barbieri, who later signed a $3 million book deal.

"For God's sake, definitely I didn't write it."

Writer Joe Klein, 1996, denying to the *New York Times* that he wrote the novel *Primary Colors.*

"I'm telling you, I didn't write it."

Joe Klein, 1996, denying to the *Washington Post* that he wrote the novel *Primary Colors.*

"It's not me. I didn't do it. This is silly."

Writer Joe Klein, February 1996, denying to CBS News that he wrote the novel *Primary Colors.* He admitted it five months later.

Worst Feet Forward

"The time may have come to say good-bye to Muhammad Ali."

Broadcaster Howard Cosell, 1974, predicting Ali's loss to heavyweight boxing champ George Foreman in their title bout in Zaire. Ali won.

"I'm twenty-four and I think I'll get a lot more opportunities."

Golfer Jerry Pate, 1978, after losing one of professional golf's major championships in 1978. Pate never won another.

"No man was great enough to come back three times. I will do it a fourth time because it's there."

Boxer Muhammad Ali, 1981, before his bid to win the heavyweight title one more time. He lost to Canadian champ Trevor Berbick in ten rounds.

"In twenty years of tournament golf involving amateurs, I've never been hit by a ball."

Golfer Hale Irwin, 1989, one week before he was hit on the head at the Los Angeles Open tournament.

"I have more faith in my wife than to bump off her competition."

Tonya Harding's husband Jeff Gillooly, January 1994, less than two months before he pleaded guilty to assaulting Harding's skating rival Nancy Kerrigan.

Better Left Unsaid

"All men are created equal."

From the Declaration of Independence, July 4, 1776, by Thomas Jefferson, a slaveowner until his death fifty years later.

"Don't give up the ship."

US Navy captain and commander of the frigate *Chesapeake* James Lawrence, 1813, in a battle with the British sea frigate HMS *Shannon*. He did, and died.

"I will give him . . . such an illumination as this world has never seen."

A priest from the Jesuit Church of La Compania, Chile, 1863, promising a glorious pageant for the visiting representative from the Pope. Unfortunately, the church burned down before the pageant began.

"You will never amount to very much."

A Munich teacher to ten-year-old Albert Einstein, 1889.

"I have no enemies. Why should I fear?"

US President William McKinley, August 1901, a few days before his assassination.

"You bet I will pull through."

Financier J.P. Morgan, 1913, upon emerging from a coma. Within minutes he was dead.

"I am very happy in the Senate and much prefer to remain there. I do not believe I could be happy as President. I don't want it."

US Senator Warren G. Harding, 1920, before running for and winning the presidency.

"Thousand-year Reich."

Slogan, *circa* 1930s, predicting the length of Nazi Party rule in Germany, which in fact lasted twelve years.

"We shall not capitulate – no, never!"

German Chancellor Adolf Hitler, 1939, six years before Germany surrendered and he killed himself.

"Don't worry about it. . . . It's nothing."

US Navy Lieutenant Kermit Tyler, December 7, 1941, upon being informed that radar had just picked up a large formation of planes heading for Hawaii. It was, of course, the first wave of the Japanese attack on Pearl Harbor.

“Fireproof.”

Designation given by Atlanta fire inspectors, 1946, to the Winecoff Hotel, which shortly thereafter burned to the ground.

“The largest, safest, and most modern hotel west of New York.”

Promotional copy for Chicago’s La Salle Hotel, which went up in flames on June 5, 1946.

"You can't say the people of Dallas haven't given you a nice welcome."

Mrs. John Connally, wife of the Governor of Texas, to President John F. Kennedy, November 22, 1963, just prior to Kennedy's assassination.

"We have a free press . . . honest elections. . . . In all this part of the world, where will democratic ways work if they fail here?"

Philippines President Ferdinand Marcos, 1967, five years before declaring martial law so as to remain in power and nineteen years before being overthrown for corruption.

"I'm going to live to be one hundred."

American health author Jerome Rodale, 1971, who died the next day at age fifty-one.

"I have no intention whatever of walking away from the job I was elected to do."

President Richard Nixon, November 1973, nine months before he resigned from office.

". . . a survivor who is frustrating the curse of the Oscar."

Washington Post profile in September 1978 of actor Gig Young, who shot his wife and himself to death a month later.

"It's too early for a Polish pope."

Polish Cardinal Karol Wojtyla, October 1978, two days before he was elected as Pope John Paul II.

"I'll keep you safe, kids. I swear to God."

Dialogue to be spoken by actor Vic Morrow, 1982, as he rescued two Vietnamese children in *Twilight Zone: The Movie*. Before the scene was shot, however, Morrow and the two child actors were killed in an on-set accident.

"I have just one father. I want to make peace with him."

Singer Marvin Gaye, 1984, shortly before he got into a fight with his dad, who shot and killed him.

"Can you believe this crap?"

Actor Jon-Erik Hexum, October 1984, before firing a gun loaded with blanks during a break in filming his television show, COVER-UP. The impact from the blast put Hexum in a coma, and he died six days later.

"You don't understand. They don't kidnap journalists."

Journalist Terry Anderson, 1985, less than a week before he was kidnapped by Arab terrorists.

"The fact is that I don't like publicity. I absolutely hate doing an interview."

Tycoon Donald Trump, 1987, in an interview with *People* magazine. Trump eventually put his name on a casino, an airline, and a bicycle race, in addition to the Trump Tower in New York City.

"I've got Bush by the balls."

Panamanian leader Manuel Noriega, 1988, on US President George Bush. Two years later Noriega was behind bars, courtesy of US forces despatched by Bush.

"The rich and famous should be judged differently. The city couldn't live with the little people's tax money."

Actress Zsa Zsa Gabor, 1989, claiming that she shouldn't be held responsible for slapping a police officer after a routine arrest. In fact, she was found guilty.

"Taxes are for the little people."

Billionairess Leona Helmsley, *circa* mid-1980s. Helmsley was subsequently convicted on charges of tax evasion.

Wishful Thinking

"Assassination can be no more guarded against than death by lightning and it is best not to worry about either."

President James A. Garfield, 1881, who was soon after assassinated.

"In 1993, the world will have become equalized in every respect, even to dire monotony."

Magazine publishing magnate Miriam Leslie, 1893. Anybody bored yet?

"The citizens who live in the next century are not going to pay two cents for a letter postage stamp. The price will be reduced to one cent."

US Postmaster-General Thomas L. James, 1893. A stamp for an ordinary letter within the United States costs 32 cents today.

"All theology will be conceded to be mythology."

Noted American journalist, author, and lawyer Van Buren Denslow, 1893, speculating on how things would look in 1993.

"Free delivery will be universal."

Postmaster-General John Wanamaker, 1893, predicting how the US postal system would look in 1993.

“Far more religion than now. . . . The spirit of religion dominant.”

American newspaper columnist and clergyman Thomas DeWitt Talmage, 1893, predicting the role of theology one hundred years in the future.

“People have got to know whether or not their President is a crook. Well, I’m not a crook. I’ve earned everything I’ve got.”

Richard M. Nixon, 1974, about the burglary of Democratic National Headquarters in the Watergate building Washington, DC.

"One hundred years hence, I think the President of the United States will have much less work on his hands than he has now."

US Army Paymaster and former personal secretary to President Benjamin Harrison, Elijah Halford, 1893.

"Men will grow wiser, better, and purer in the years to come."

US Senator William A. Peffer, 1893, predicting how things would look in 1993.

"Transcontinental mails will be forwarded by means of pneumatic tubes."

Renowned American writer and naturalist Felix Oswald, 1893, predicting how the world would look in 1993.

"Not just another war – it is the last war."

British historian and author H.G. Wells, 1914, speaking about the first – and hardly the last – world war.

"I have seen over into the future, and it works."

American journalist Lincoln Steffens, 1919, upon returning from a trip to post-Revolution Russia.

"England is at last ripe for revolution."

Russian Communist leader Leon Trotsky, 1925, predicting the overthrow of the British government.

"In thirty years the United States will see the end of dire poverty, distress, and unnecessary suffering."

Real-estate mogul and philanthropist August Heckscher, 1930. Still waiting.

"I do not believe in the probability of anything much worse than mustard gas being produced."

British scientist J.B.S. Haldane, 1937, on the future of weaponry.

“No enemy bomber can reach the Ruhr.”

Nazi leader and head of the Luftwaffe Hermann Goering, 1939, on the impossibility that enemy aircraft could penetrate into Germany.

“It’s a phoney war.”

French prime minister Édouard Daladier, 1939, on the beginning of World War II.

"In the course of thirty years the human race will have been biologically restored. It will come into the world without any trace of fascist distortion."

Austrian psychiatrist Wilhelm Reich, 1946.

"[Television] won't be able to hold on to any market it captures after the first six months. People will soon get tired of staring at a plywood box every night."

Twentieth-Century Fox studio boss Darryl F. Zanuck, 1946.

"The housewife of 2000 can do her daily cleaning with a garden hose."

Popular Mechanics magazine, 1950, predicting that U.S. homes and all their furnishings would be made of plastic by the end of the century.

"I found nothing but progress and hope for the future."

US Secretary of Defense Robert McNamara, 1963, upon returning from a visit to Vietnam. American involvement in the Vietnam War was to continue for another ten years.

"I'm not going to lose Vietnam."

US President Lyndon B. Johnson, 1963.

"Within ten to twenty years' time we could have a robot that will completely eliminate all routine operations around the house and remove the drudgery from human life."

British mechanical-engineering professor Meredith Woolridge Thring, 1964.

"The major part of the US Military task in Vietnam can be completed by the end of 1965."

US Secretary of Defense Robert McNamara, 1965. He was off by just eight years in time, and an entire ideology in outcome.

"A normal aberration."

Three Mile Island nuclear-power-plant spokesman Jack Herbein, 1979, in the early stages of the most serious nuclear disaster in US history.

"High standards start here. Rigourous Graduation Requirement. Mathematics and Writing Proficiencey Exams."

Newspaper ad for Milwaukee's public-school system, 1997, in which the words "rigorous" and "proficiency" were misspelled.

"We've built a yellow-brick road to the summit."

Mountain climber Scott Fischer before a fateful ascent of Mount Everest in 1996 that resulted in eight deaths, including his own.

Sources and Bibliography

The quotations in this collection were gleaned from the books listed below, as well as from a variety of publications and periodicals, including (but not limited to) *Entertainment Weekly*, the *National Review*, the *New Republic*, the *New York Times*, *Newsweek*, *People*, *Smart Money* and *Time*. The editor gratefully acknowledges all assistance in compiling the material for this book, especially that of Jason Zweig at *Money*.

Edward Angly. *Oh Yeah?* New York: Viking, 1931.

Louise K. Barnett. *Touched by Fire: The Life, Death, and Mythic Afterlife of George Armstrong Custer*. New York: Henry Holt, 1996.

Edward Behr. *Hirohito: Behind the Myth*. New York: Villard Books, 1989.

Andre Bernard, ed. *Rotten Rejections*. Wainscott, N.Y.: Pushcart Press, 1990.

Wilford Binkley. *President and Congress*. New York: Vintage Books, 1962.

Ivan F. Boesky. *Merger Mania*. New York: Holt, Rinehart and Winston, 1985.

Paul F. Boller, Jr. *Quotemanship*. Dallas: Southern Methodist University Press, 1967.

Connie Bruck. *The Predator's Ball*. New York: Simon and Schuster, 1988.

James M. Burns. *Roosevelt: The Soldier of Freedom*. New York: Harcourt Brace Jovanovich, 1970.

Bob Chieger and Pat Sullivan. *Football's Greatest Quotes*. New York: Simon and Schuster, 1990.

Winston Churchill. *The Second World War, II, Their Finest Hour*. New York: Bantam Books, 1962.

Joseph Corn and Brian Horrigan. *Yesterday's Tomorrows: Past Visions of the American Future*. Baltimore: Johns Hopkins University Press, 1975.

Deborah Davis Eisel and Jill Swanson, eds. *Dictionary of Contemporary Quotations*. New York: John Gordon Burke Publisher, 1981.

Stuart Flexner with Doris Flexner. *The Pessimist's Guide to History*. New York: Hearst Books, 1992.

Frank Friedel. *Franklin D. Roosevelt*. Boston: Little, Brown, 1956.

Elizabeth Frost, ed. *The World Almanac of Presidential Quotations*. New York: Pharos Books, 1988.

Jonathan Green, ed. *The Book of Political Quotes*. New York: McGraw-Hill, 1982.

Jeff Greenfield. *The Real Campaign*. New York: Summit Books, 1982.

Martin Gilbert. *The First World War: A Complete History*. New York: Henry Holt, 1994.

Charles F. Hemphill Jr. *Famous Phrases From History. Jefferson*, NC: McFarland & Co., 1982.

Bill Henderson, ed. *Rotten Reviews*. New York: Pushcart Press, 1986.

Herman Kahn and Anthony J. Weiner. *The Year 2000: A Framework for Speculation on the Next Thirty-Three Years*. New York: Macmillan, 1967.

Ken Janke. *Golf Is a Funny Game – But It Wasn't Meant to Be*. Ann Arbor, Mich.: Momentum Books, 1992.

David G. McCullough. *Truman*. New York: Simon and Schuster, 1992.

H.L. Mencken, ed. *A New Dictionary of Quotations, on Historical Principles*. New York: Knopf, 1957.

Janice Peck. *The Gods of Televangelism*. Cresskill, NJ: Hampton Press, 1993.

Jospeh E. Persico. *The Imperial Rockefeller*. New York: Simon and Schuster, 1982.

Stephen Pile. *The Art of Being Wrong*. London: Futura Publications, 1980.

Suzy Platt, ed. *Respectfully Quoted: A Dictionary of Quotations From the Library of Congress*. Washington, DC: Congressional Quarterly, 1992.

Nicholas Schaffner. *The Beatles Forever*. Harrisburg, Penn.: Cameron House, 1977.

Robert Sobel. *Panic on Wall Street*. New York: Macmillan, 1968.

Janet Street-Porter. *Scandal*. New York: Dell, 1981.

Michael C. Thomsett. *War and Conflict Quotations: A Worldwide History of Pronouncements from Military Leaders, Politicians, Philosophers, Writers and Others*. Jefferson, NC: McFarland & Co., 1997.

Michael Valenti. *Sports Quotes*. New York: Facts on File, 1983.

If you would like more information on the full list of humour titles published by Michael O'Mara Books Limited please contact our UK sales department on:

fax: 0171 622 6956
e-mail: *jokes@michaelomarabooks.com*

Titles include:

- *The Complete History of Farting*
- *The World's Greatest Lies*
- *Bitch!*
- *The Stupidest Things Ever Said*
- *The Stupidest Things Ever Done*
- *Stupid Sex*
- *The Nastiest Things Ever Said*